The Good Food Cookbook
for Dogs

Merry Christmas Nicole!
Feed your Majic these
deeelicious recipies,
as I love them too!
Love,
Corky
XMAS 2008

QUARRY

The Good Food Cookbook *for* Dogs

GLOUCESTER MASSACHUSETTS

QUARRY BOOKS

50 Home-Cooked Recipes
for the Health and Happiness
of Your Canine Companion

Donna Twichell Roberts

First published in the United States of America by
Quarry Books, an imprint of
Rockport Publishers, Inc.
33 Commercial Street
Gloucester, Massachusetts 01930-5089
Telephone: (978) 282-9590
Fax: (978) 283-2742
www.rockpub.com

Library of Congress Cataloging-in-Publication Data

Roberts, Donna Twichell.
    The good food cookbook for dogs : 50 home-cooked recipes for the
health and happiness of your canine companion / Donna Twichell Roberts.
        p.   cm.
    ISBN 1-59253-067-2 (pbk.)
    1. Dogs—Food—Recipes. I. Title.
SF427.4.R63 2004
636.7'0855—dc22   2004008831
                                                          CIP

Neither the publisher nor the author accepts liability for the suitability of
the recipes in this cookbook for the health of individual dogs. Homemade
food should be given to a dog at the owner's discretion, and dogs should be
under veterinary care. While every attempt has been made to present and
apply the basic principles of canine nutrition, this is a cookbook and is not
intended to be a text or resource on canine nutrition.

ISBN: 1-59253-067-2

10 9 8 7 6 5 4 3 2

All recipes © Donna Twichell Roberts
Photographs on pages 4–5, 6, 9, 10, 18, 36, 38, 48, 56, 58, 60, 64, 78, 92,
96, 98, 108, 110, 120, 122, 129, and 130, Getty Images
Photograph on page 132 © Laurie Klein
All other photography by Tony Scarpetta Photography
Design: Art & Anthropology
Cover Image: Blake Little / Getty Images

Printed in Singapore

To my father, Lewis
Twichell, who has always
had a soft spot for dogs.
And to my daughter,
Adria, who carries on
the dog-loving DNA.
In loving memory of
Humphrey and Gwennie.

"What Goes With What...?"

<u>Westie White Sauce</u> (pg. 54), goes with...

Tuna Noodle Casserole – pg. 40

Turkey Croquettes – pg. 45

Beef Stroganoff Sauce – pg. 55

Chicken-a-la-King – pg. 57

Four Cheese Sauce – pg. 57

<u>Four Cheese Sauce</u> (pg.57), goes with...

Mac 'N' Cheese with Sausage – pg. 41

Tuna Melt – pg. 59

<u>Giblet Gravy</u> (pg. 53), goes by itself,
just add to dry food.

<u>Lip-Lickin' Liver-Lover's Sauce</u> (pg. 54), goes with...

Liver Lips – pg. 75

CONTENTS

If you love to cook and you love dogs, pretty soon you are cooking *for* dogs. At least, that is what happened to me.

More than fifteen years ago, a friend gave me a recipe for "dog stew" that her vet had given her. It was a mixture of chicken and canned vegetables. I tried it, just for the fun of it. My dog loved it, of course, and I never again opened a can of dog food. (Well, almost never.) Since then, I have cooked for all my dogs—Humphrey and Gwennie, and now Katie—West Highland White Terriers, the breed of dog that owns my heart. Other beneficiaries of my home cooking are Casey the Cairn Terrier, my foster dog for one year, as well as Roux, my big dopey "granddog," whenever he comes to visit.

The original recipe for "dog stew" evolved into Chicken 'n' Rice Stew; then the repertoire expanded to include Beef Barley Stew and others.

The original recipe for "dog stew" evolved into Chicken 'n' Rice Stew (page 21); then the repertoire expanded to include Beef Barley Stew (page 23) and others. Anyone who has ever shared a bit of Thanksgiving dinner with a dog—a little turkey, mashed potatoes, gravy, maybe even a little stuffing—knows that dogs love much of the same food their people enjoy. Yet our veterinarians admonish us not to feed our dogs table scraps. So, I decided I would develop recipes based on home-cooked "people" favorites, adapted for dogs. The chapter on nutrition (chapter 1, "Good Nutrition for Dogs," page 11) will provide some of the basics of dog nutrition so you have a better understanding of what your dog needs. You will also find some basic guidelines for developing your own recipes.

INTRODUCTION

In this book you will find all my recipes for everyday dinners (chapter 2, "Stews and Casseroles," page 19) plus sauces to pour over your dog's regular food (chapter 3, "Gravies and Sauces," page 49). There are homemade goodies for the cookie jar (chapter 4, "Savory Snacks," page 61; chapter 5, "Sweet Treats," page 79). For festive occasions, turn to chapter 6, "Party and Holiday Food" (page 93) for recipes, ideas, and ways to celebrate with your dog. There is also a chapter on "Ethnic Specialties" (chapter 7, page 111) as well as one on "Special Diets for Special Needs" (chapter 8, page 123).

All recipes have been developed under the careful and constant supervision of Katie and taste-tested by an assortment of dogs, large and small, purebred and purely mutt, all of whom had paws-itive praise for my canine culinary efforts.

Whether you make one recipe or try all of them, I hope you enjoy cooking for your dog. I know your dog will enjoy your cooking because, perhaps unlike your human family, dogs don't mind eating the same thing night after night. They never say, "Not this again." They will be waiting for their dinner just as eagerly as Bella the bulldog on the cover is.

What more could a cook ask for?

CHAPTER 1

GOOD NUTRITION FOR DOGS

There are lots of good reasons to cook for your dog:

To provide a healthy diet based on fresh ingredients,
To meet his special needs and accommodate his taste preferences,
To nurture him as you would any other member of the family.

Provide Nutritious Food

Good nutrition is, of course, the basic reason to cook food for your dog. But let's face it, your dog can get good nutrition from a can or a bag. Decades of veterinary research have gone into perfecting a complete and balanced meal in a convenient form for your dog.

Theoretically, you cannot improve upon commercially available dog food, which is tested, inspected, and government regulated. Furthermore, canine nutrition is highly complex. Different combinations of nutrients are required at different developmental stages, from puppies to ailing seniors, from nursing mothers to special-purpose dogs such as sled dogs. Some breeds even have their own specific nutritional needs. The recipes in this book are just that—recipes. While they are not scientific formulas, they are based on general nutrition guidelines for healthy adult dogs. They are intended to be served as part of a dog's complete diet in conjunction with commercial dry dog food.

I think it *is* important to combine home-cooked food with high-quality dry dog food. First of all, making your own dry dog food is nearly impossible. Believe me, I have tried, and it was probably the only thing my dogs refused to eat. Dogs need hard crunchies to keep their teeth and gums in good shape. Combining dry dog food with your own homemade stews ensures that your dog gets all his nutrients. Veterinarians also recommend giving your dog a vitamin and mineral supplement.

When you cook for your dog, you know what is in the food you make. It will have few to no additives or preservatives because you are using mostly fresh ingredients. You may also decide to use only organic ingredients for the recipes if you are so inclined.

And, of course, you will not find "animal by-products" in your own homemade food. This alone is a compelling reason to cook for your dog. Animal by-products as a category are not pleasant for dog lovers to think about. By-products include chicken beaks, arteries, skin, and other parts. When ground up, they are probably harmless to the dog. But many people believe that by-products include diseased animal parts, and this, of course, goes beyond unappetizing to scary.

Meet Special Needs

Beyond good nutrition, you can satisfy other needs—your own and the dog's—by making homemade dog food.

Some dogs have special needs brought on by ailments, disease, or other conditions. You can still cook for the dog on a special diet, supplementing his food with prescriptive dry dog food you buy at the vet's. Ensuring that your dog gets an appetizing meal made from fresh ingredients is one way to put him back on the trail to good health.

Few dogs are finicky, though many still prefer some foods over others. If your dog spits out the green beans in one recipe, try substituting another green vegetable that he likes. Another dog will let you know that lamb is, by far, his favorite meat and would be happy if you cooked nothing but the Lamb and Brown Rice Stew (page 27). Other dogs will be happy to have you start cooking at the beginning of the book and not stop until you get to the end. They will eat everything with equal enthusiasm. You will learn what your dog's taste preferences are because he will find a way to let you know.

Nurture Your Dog

In addition to providing your dog with nutritious, homemade food; meeting his special needs; and satisfying his taste preferences, home cooking lets you nurture your dog with the same love and care that you lavish on the human members of your family (maybe more!).

Makeup of a Healthy Main Dish

Remember, stews and casseroles comprise your dog's main meal when combined with dry dog food. Most canine nutrition experts agree that dogs need:

PROTEIN from beef, pork, lamb, poultry, game, and fish as well as eggs, milk, soy, legumes, and corn. Protein sources contain the ten essential amino acids required by dogs. No one protein source provides all the essential amino acids, however, so giving your dog food containing a variety of protein foods is beneficial.

CARBOHYDRATE from rice, potatoes, pasta, barley, and other grains as well as vegetables and fruits. Carbohydrates, including high-fiber foods, are a source of energy, add bulk to help a dog feel full, and provide roughage to help keep the digestive system functioning properly.

FAT from vegetable oil, other oil, and fat naturally present in meat. One of the fatty acids, linoleic acid found in vegetable oil, is essential to dogs. It provides energy and may help fight inflammation.

VITAMINS AND MINERALS from vegetables and fruits as well as other ingredients. Although veterinarians recommend giving dogs a vitamin and mineral supplement, fresh fruits and vegetables contain many micronutrients not found in a typical supplement and can work together to benefit a dog's overall good health.

If you want to know more about canine nutrition, you should consult one of the publications listed in the Resources on page 131. Also, make sure that your dog is under a veterinarian's care to help ensure that his diet, whether homemade or commercially prepared, meets all his nutritional needs.

How Much to Feed

How much food to give your dog each day depends, of course, on his age, weight, and activity level. Here are some general guidelines for a healthy adult dog:

Weight

Recommended Daily Amount

3 to 10 pounds (1.4 to 4.5 kg)

⅓ cup to ¾ cup (75 to 170 g)

11 to 20 pounds (5 to 9 kg)

¾ cup to 1⅛ cups (170 to 250 g)

21 to 30 pounds (9.5 to 13.6 kg)

1⅛ cups to 1½ cups (250 to 340 g)

31 to 40 pounds (14 to 18 kg)

1½ cups to 1¾ cups (340 to 395 g)

41 to 60 pounds (18.6 to 27 kg)

1¾ cups to 2⅓ cups (395 to 525 g)

61 to 80 pounds (27.7 to 36 kg)

2⅓ cups to 3 cups (525 to 675 g)

81 to 100 pounds (36.7 to 45.4 kg)

3 cups to 3¾ cups (675 to 845 g)

101 pounds and up (45.8 kg and up)

3¾ cups to 6 cups (845 to 990 g)

Make-Your-Own-Stew Matrix

Once you have tried a few of the stew and other main-dish recipes provided in this cookbook, you will probably find several that you will make on a regular basis.

In the process, you will learn about your dog's taste preferences such as whether he prefers beef to chicken, carrots more than squash, or green beans over peas.

At that point, you may wish to tailor a recipe specifically for your dog's likes. Here is a basic guideline for doing so:

For about 8 quarts (7.6 L) of stew,

YOU NEED	CHOOSE FROM
≈1 pound (450 g) protein	Beef, pork, lamb, mild sausage, chicken, turkey, fish or seafood, cheese
≈6 cups (990 g) cooked grains	Rice (including brown rice), barley, oatmeal
≈4 to 6 cups (840 to 990 g) "starchy" carbohydrate	Potatoes (including red and Yukon Gold), yams and sweet potatoes, pasta, bread
≈6 to 8 cups (990 g to 1.2 kg) vegetables and/or fruits	Carrots; celery; cabbage; green beans; peas; squash (including zucchini); spinach and other leafy greens such as kale, chard, collard; turnips or rutabagas; apples; pears
≈3 to 4 quarts (2.8 to 3.8 L) liquid	Beef, chicken, or vegetable broth; canned tomatoes with juice; milk; water
≈2 to 4 tablespoons fat	Vegetable oil (including soybean, canola, and sunflower oils), olive oil, naturally occurring fats from meat, poultry, and fish

Introducing New Food

If your dog is going from canned food to homemade, he is going to be very happy.

Unless he has a particularly sensitive stomach, he should have no problem going right from what he has been eating to one of the stew recipes. I have started an eight-week-old puppy on Chicken 'n' Rice Stew (page 20). I fed my dog who lived in good health to the venerable age of sixteen the stew recipes throughout his life. And I have fed rescue and foster dogs the stews. Stews are always mixed with the appropriate dry dog food, of course. No dog ever had a problem going from whatever it was eating to homemade food.

If you want to transition your dog slowly from its current food to homemade, however, do so by substituting one-quarter of his regular moist food with the homemade food. Every couple of days, increase the proportion of homemade food and decrease the regular moist food until you are certain that your dog's digestive system can handle it properly.

Caution about Controversy

Just as doctors and dietitians cannot agree on what foods are best for humans, not everyone agrees on what is best to feed dogs.

And few topics can get dog lovers embroiled in an argument like what to feed their dogs. From those who feed their dogs canned and packaged dog food to those who have their dogs on the BARF (bones and raw food) diet, all love their dogs and have their best interest in mind. You know your dog best—what he likes, what he needs, and how he feels. Feed him accordingly.

Water, Water

Water is your dog's most important nutrient. Water makes up 70 percent of an adult dog's weight. Your dog cannot live without water. In fact, a dog can die within a few days if he becomes dehydrated. Always make sure your dog has access to plenty of clean, good-quality water.

CHAPTER 2

STEWS AND CASSEROLES

Stews and casseroles are designed to be the main dishes of your dog's diet. Made fresh and served warm, these dinnertime recipes are home cooking for dogs at its most delicious. This is not fast food. After all, if you wanted fast food for your dog, you would open a can. Instead, you want your dog to have the best.

Do not be surprised if your canine companion keeps you company while you cook. No one, especially a dog with a nose for good food, can resist the aroma of home-cooked stew simmering on the stove or a casserole right out of the oven.

Doggerel

This is the first "meal" I ever cooked for my dogs. It started when a friend gave me a recipe for chicken stew from her vet. I tried it and, of course, my dog at the time—Humphrey, a West Highland White Terrier of great dignity and more than a few weird ways—loved it. That was more than fifteen years ago, and I have never looked back.

This recipe has evolved over the years and resembles the original recipe only in that it is still a chicken stew recipe. The original recipe used almost all canned vegetables. I use fresh vegetables to the extent possible but also rely on frozen vegetables as well as canned goods such as tomatoes and broth. So, by all means, use canned or frozen vegetables if that makes your life easier. Whether you serve one recipe exclusively or rotate it with one or more other recipes, your dog will think all are his favorites.

TIP

Whenever you roast a chicken or turkey, save the giblets and freeze. Sauté them in a little oil—either separately, stirring them into the stew at the end, or in the stockpot first thing— then proceed with stew preparation from step 2. Or, use them to make Giblet Gravy (page 53).

I should caution you that the aroma of freshly made stew is as irresistible to people as it is to dogs. Anytime I make a batch of stew for my dogs, my daughter and I also sit down to a bowl. Add a little salt and pepper, grate some cheese over the top, and you have yourself a mighty fine meal. The dogs will be too busy chowing down on their own supper to notice that you are digging into the stewpot.

Think of this as Sunday chicken dinner for your dog. He won't get tired of it even if you serve it every night of the week.

INGREDIENTS

One 2½-pound (1.1 kg) package chicken legs (about 6 legs)*

2 quarts (1.9 L) water, divided

1 cup (200 g) rice

One 28-ounce (828 ml) can diced tomatoes in juice

One 28-ounce (828 ml) can chicken broth

4 potatoes, peeled and chopped

4 carrots, peeled and sliced

1 cup (150 g) macaroni

One 24-ounce (680 g) package frozen peas

*Or, use 1 package skinless, boneless chicken breasts (about 4 breasts), cut into bite-sized pieces, or use 1½ to 2 pounds (675 to 900 g) ground chicken. Sauté chicken pieces or ground chicken in 1 tablespoon vegetable oil in an 8-quart (7.6 L) stockpot and proceed with recipe as directed from step 2.

CHICKEN 'N' RICE STEW

DIRECTIONS

1 Place chicken legs in a baking dish and place in a preheated 375°F (190°C) oven. Roast for 30 minutes, then turn chicken legs and roast an additional 15 to 20 minutes. When slightly cooled, remove meat from bones and set aside. Meanwhile, add enough water to cover drippings in the baking dish; return to oven for 10 to 15 minutes. Remove from oven. Using a spoon, loosen any brown bits on bottom or sides of pan. Reserve this liquid. (Bones may be discarded or wrapped and frozen to be cooked into chicken broth later.) This step can be done a day ahead or early in the day.

2 Bring 2 cups (450 ml) water to boil over high heat in a 3-quart (2.8 L) saucepan. Add rice, reduce heat to medium-low, cover, and cook for 15 to 20 minutes until all water has been absorbed. Set aside.

3 Meanwhile, place tomatoes with juice, remaining 6 cups (1.4 L) water, and chicken broth in an 8-quart (7.6 L) stockpot. Bring to boil over high heat.

4 Add potatoes and carrots. Reduce heat to medium-high and cook, stirring occasionally, for 10 minutes.

5 Add macaroni and cook, stirring frequently, for an additional 10 minutes.

6 Remove from heat and stir in peas, cooked rice, cooked chicken, and any reserved liquid. Makes 8 quarts (7.6 L). (Recipe may be doubled.)

Storing and Serving Stew

- Allow stew to cool somewhat in the pan; then ladle into 1-quart (0.95 L) freezer containers or 1-quart (0.95 L) zipper-style plastic bags. Refrigerate overnight, preferably in a single layer, before placing in the freezer.

- Each 8-quart (7.6 L) batch of stew will make enough for four to eight weeks' worth of dinners for one dog, depending on size.

- To thaw, remove package from the freezer two to three days ahead of time and place in the refrigerator. Or, early in the day, place package in water just up to but not covering the rim. Refrigerate when thawed.

- Keep thawed stew in the refrigerator at all times.

- At mealtime, portion the amount you want into a dog bowl and microwave on high about 30 to 45 seconds for ½ cup (120 g). Mix with dry dog food and serve.

- Use about one part stew to four parts dry dog food.

Beef and barley make a classic combination that dogs, always meat lovers, can barely wait to devour.

BEEF BARLEY STEW

INGREDIENTS

2 quarts (1.9 L) water, divided

1 cup (185 g) barley

1 tablespoon vegetable oil

1 pound (450 g) ground beef*

One 28-ounce (828 ml) can diced tomatoes in juice

1 quart (0.95 L) beef broth

4 potatoes, peeled and chopped

4 carrots, peeled and sliced

1 cup (150 g) macaroni

1 small head cabbage, quartered and thinly sliced

* Or, use 1 pound (450 g) boneless beef, cut into bite-sized pieces.

DIRECTIONS

1 Bring 2½ cups (565 ml) water to boil over high heat in a 3-quart (2.8 L) saucepan. Add barley, reduce heat to medium-low, cover, and cook for 45 to 50 minutes until all water has been absorbed. Set aside.

2 Heat oil in an 8-quart (7.6 L) stockpot over medium-high heat. Add beef and cook, stirring frequently, until meat is brown, about 8 minutes.

3 Add tomatoes with juice, remaining 5½ cups (1.3 L) water, and beef broth. Bring to boil over high heat.

4 Add potatoes and carrots. Reduce heat to medium-high and cook, stirring occasionally, for 10 minutes.

5 Add macaroni and cook, stirring frequently, for an additional 10 minutes.

6 Remove from heat and stir in cabbage and cooked barley. Makes 8 quarts (7.6 L). (Recipe may be doubled.)

TIP

To make it easier to cut beef into bite-sized pieces, divide the meat into four pieces. Wrap individual pieces in plastic wrap and place in freezer for 20 to 30 minutes. Remove pieces, one at a time; unwrap; and cut into bite-sized pieces. Because the meat is somewhat frozen, it will cut more easily. Repeat until all meat is cut.

Large dogs
(over 50 pounds [23 kg])

Medium dogs
(26 to 50 pounds [11.5 to 23 kg])

Small dogs
(10 to 25 pounds [4.5 to 11.5 kg])

"Bite-sized" means one thing to a Lhasa Apso and quite another to a Labrador Retriever. This guide will help you decide what size to cut meat and vegetables for your dog.

Toy breeds
(under 10 pounds [4.5 kg])

Though somewhat pricey, lamb is a flavorful alternative to beef, and a favorite of dogs. Brown rice adds to this stew's good-nutrition quotient.

LAMB AND BROWN RICE STEW

DIRECTIONS

1 Bring 2½ cups (565 ml) water to boil over high heat in a 3-quart (2.8 L) saucepan. Add brown rice, reduce heat to medium-low, cover, and cook for 45 to 50 minutes until all water has been absorbed. Set aside.

2 Meanwhile, remove lamb meat from bone and cut into bite-sized pieces. Set aside. (After you have removed as much meat from the bones as possible, you may place lamb bones in a baking dish in a preheated 425°F (220°C) oven and bake until brown, about 30 minutes. Remove cooked meat from bones and set aside. Discard bones.)

3 Heat oil in an 8-quart (7.6 L) stockpot over medium-high heat. Add lamb and cook, stirring frequently, until meat is brown, about 5 to 8 minutes.

4 Add tomatoes with juice, remaining 5½ cups (1.3 L) water, and beef broth. Bring to boil over high heat.

5 Add turnips. Reduce heat to medium-high, and cook 5 minutes.

6 Add potatoes, carrots, and lentils. Cook, stirring occasionally, for an additional 20 minutes.

7 Remove from heat and stir in peas, cooked brown rice, and any of the reserved roasted lamb meat. Makes 8 quarts (7.6 L). (Recipe may be doubled.)

INGREDIENTS

2 quarts (1.9 L) water, divided

1 cup (200 g) uncooked brown rice

One 3-pound (1.4 kg) package lamb shoulder chops*

1 tablespoon vegetable oil

One 28-ounce (828 ml) can diced tomatoes in juice

1 quart (0.95 L) beef broth

4 turnips, peeled and chopped

4 potatoes, peeled and chopped

4 carrots, peeled and sliced

1 cup (225 g) lentils, rinsed

One 24-ounce (680 g) package frozen peas

* Or, use an equivalent amount of another bone-in cut of lamb or 1 pound (450 g) ground lamb.

Full of great fall flavors, this recipe will be a year-round favorite.

PORK APPLE STEW

INGREDIENTS

2 quarts (1.9 L) water, divided

1 cup (200 g) uncooked brown rice

2 acorn squash

2 tablespoons vegetable oil, divided

1 pound (450 g) pork,* cut into bite-sized pieces

One 28-ounce (828 ml) can diced tomatoes in juice

1 quart (0.95 L) chicken broth

4 potatoes, preferably Yukon Gold, peeled and chopped

2 cups (150 g) medium egg noodles

1 small head cabbage, quartered and thinly sliced

2 apples, chopped

*Or, use ground pork.

DIRECTIONS

1 Bring 2½ cups (565 ml) water to boil over high heat in a 3-quart (2.8 L) saucepan. Add brown rice, reduce heat to medium-low, cover, and cook 45 to 50 minutes until all water has been absorbed. Set aside.

2 Cut acorn squash in half horizontally and scoop out seeds. Use 1 tablespoon of oil to cover the cut edges and place squash, cut-side down, on foil-lined baking sheet. Bake in a preheated 350°F (180°C) oven for 30 to 35 minutes until just tender. Remove from oven. When slightly cool, scoop out squash. Coarsely chop, if necessary. Set aside.

3 Meanwhile, heat remaining oil in 8-quart (7.6 L) stockpot over medium-high heat. Add pork and cook, stirring frequently, until meat is brown, 4 to 6 minutes.

4 Add tomatoes with juice, remaining 5½ cups (1.3 L) water, and chicken broth. Bring to boil over high heat.

5 Add potatoes. Reduce heat to medium-high and cook, stirring occasionally, for 5 minutes.

6 Add noodles and cook, stirring frequently, for an additional 5 minutes.

7 Remove from heat and stir in cabbage, squash, apples, and cooked rice. Makes about 8 quarts (7.6 L). (Recipe may be doubled.) Garnish with doggie or piggy croutons, if desired.

To make doggie or piggy croutons, use a cookie cutter to cut dog or pig shapes out of bread slices. Fry bread cutouts in oil over medium-high heat in small skillet until brown on both sides, about 1 minute total.

What dog hasn't wished he could take a bite out of a cat? Well, here is his chance! Loaded with such favorite Southern ingredients as yams and collard greens, this recipe will appeal to Dixie dogs and Yankee Poodles alike.

INGREDIENTS

2 quarts (1.9 L) water, divided

2 cups (400 g) uncooked white rice

1 quart (0.95 L) chicken broth

4 potatoes, peeled and chopped

4 yams or sweet potatoes, peeled and chopped

1 pound (450 g) catfish fillets, cut into bite-sized pieces

2 cups (450 ml) milk

One 24-ounce (680 g) package frozen chopped collard greens, mustard greens, turnip greens, or spinach

Okay, these are really just cornbread croutons, but it's more fun to call them hushpuppies!

INGREDIENTS

1 egg, slightly beaten

⅓ cup (75 ml) milk

One 8½-ounce (241 g) package corn muffin mix

CATFISH CHOWDER WITH HUSHPUPPIES

DIRECTIONS

1 Bring 1 quart (0.95 L) water to boil over high heat in a 3-quart (2.8 L) saucepan. Add rice, reduce heat to medium-low, cover, and cook 15 to 20 minutes until all water has been absorbed. Set aside.

2 Meanwhile, place remaining 1 quart (0.95 L) water and chicken broth in an 8-quart (7.6 L) stockpot. Bring to boil over high heat.

3 Add potatoes and yams. Reduce heat to medium-high and cook, stirring occasionally, for 10 minutes.

4 Add catfish and cook, stirring occasionally, for an additional 4 to 6 minutes.

5 Remove from heat and stir in milk, collard greens, and cooked rice. Serve with hushpuppies (recipe below). Makes about 8 quarts (7.6 L). (Recipe may be doubled.)

HUSHPUPPIES

DIRECTIONS

1 Place all ingredients in a large bowl and whisk to combine. Pour into a greased 8-inch (20 cm) square baking pan. Bake in a preheated 400°F (200°C) oven for 20 minutes or until done. Let cool completely in pan.

2 Cut cornbread into quarters, then cut each quarter into 16 pieces. Store hushpuppies in airtight container or zipper-style plastic bag at room temperature. Makes 64.

Dogs rave about this dinnertime medley with two kinds of potato. In fact, dogs think the word "rave" is short for "ravenous," which they always are when they smell sausage cooking.

KIELBASA-POTATO DINNER

INGREDIENTS

1 tablespoon vegetable oil

One 1-pound (450 g) package kielbasa sausage, cut into bite-sized pieces

1 quart (0.95 L) beef broth

1 quart (0.95 L) water

12 potatoes, peeled and sliced

8 yams or sweet potatoes, peeled and sliced

One 24-ounce (680 g) package frozen cut green beans or Italian green beans

DIRECTIONS

1 Heat oil in an 8-quart (7.6 L) stockpot over medium-high heat. Add kielbasa and cook, stirring occasionally, until meat is warm throughout and beginning to brown, about 5 to 8 minutes.

2 Using a slotted spoon, transfer kielbasa from pan to paper towel–lined plate. Set aside.

3 Add just enough broth to cover bottom of pot and stir to loosen any brown bits. Add water and remaining broth. Bring to boil over high heat.

4 Add potatoes and yams. Reduce heat to medium-high and cook, stirring occasionally, for 10 minutes.

5 Remove from heat and stir in green beans and kielbasa. Makes about 8 quarts (7.6 L). (Recipe may be doubled.)

"Let the good times roll!"
Whether your dog's idea of a good time is chasing butterflies or flying saucer disks, reward his energetic efforts with a canine adaptation of this Cajun specialty.

INGREDIENTS

5 cups (1.2 L) water, divided

1 cup (200 g) uncooked white rice

1 tablespoon vegetable oil

½ pound (225 g) chicken breast, cut into bite-sized pieces (about ½ a large chicken breast)

¼ pound (115 g) ham, chopped

3 cups (675 ml) chicken broth

One 14½-ounce (429 ml) can diced tomatoes in juice

4 carrots, peeled and sliced

4 celery stalks, sliced

One 1-pound (450 g) package frozen cut okra

2 cups (300 g) small shell-shaped pasta

¼ pound (115 g) peeled and deveined medium shrimp, cut into bite-sized pieces

CHICKEN GUMBO

DIRECTIONS

1 Bring 2 cups (450 ml) water to boil over high heat in a 3-quart (2.8 L) saucepan. Add rice, reduce heat to medium-low, cover, and cook for 15 to 20 minutes until all water has been absorbed. Set aside.

2 Meanwhile, heat oil in 8-quart (7.6 L) stockpot over medium-high heat. Add chicken and ham and cook, stirring frequently, until chicken loses pink color, about 2 to 3 minutes.

3 Add chicken broth, tomatoes with juice, and remaining 3 cups (675 ml) water. Bring to boil over high heat.

4 Add carrots, celery, and okra. Reduce heat to medium-high and cook, stirring occasionally, for 5 minutes.

5 Add pasta and cook, stirring frequently, for 10 minutes.

6 Add shrimp and cook 2 minutes.

7 Remove from heat and stir in cooked rice. Makes about 8 quarts (7.6 L).

If breakfast is our most important meal, why
should a dog have to wait until 5 or 6 o'clock
at night to eat? Think how you would feel if
you ate only once a day!

Dogs can benefit from a little breakfast, too.
Breakfast helps

- Keep dogs alert and energetic throughout the day.

- Prevent "yellow throw-up"—that greenish/yellowish bile that is usually caused by having an empty stomach.

Of course, dogs should never be given more than the recommended amount of food for their weight. So subtract the amount given at breakfast from the total amount of food you give your dog.

Here are some breakfast suggestions for your dog's early-morning enjoyment:

- Just a little dry dog food

- Scrambled egg

- Cooked oatmeal with brown sugar, honey, or maple syrup

- Waffles or french toast, cut into bite-sized pieces and served with a little maple syrup or honey

- Pancakes, cut into bite-sized pieces (For an extra-special treat, use a teaspoon or tablespoon—depending on size of dog—to ladle pancake batter onto a hot griddle. Serve the bite-sized pancakes with maple syrup or honey.)

- Bone-ifried Bread (page 39)

This is the doggy version of Toad-in-a-Hole.

BONE-IFRIED BREAD

DIRECTIONS

1 Place a 3- to 4-inch (7.5 to 10 cm) bone-shaped cookie cutter on the diagonal on a piece of bread; press down and cut out. (Save cut-out bread pieces in a zipper-style plastic bag. Toast or fry another day and serve to your dog alongside a scrambled egg.)

2 Melt butter in a skillet over medium-high heat. Place bread slice in pan, then carefully pour enough of the egg into the bone-shaped cutout to fill it (about half the egg).

3 Reduce heat to medium and cook about 2 minutes on one side, then flip and cook 1 to 2 minutes on the other side until egg is set. Let cool slightly, then serve, cut into bite-sized pieces, if necessary.

INGREDIENTS

1 slice bread

1 tablespoon butter or margarine

1 egg, slightly beaten*

*One egg is enough to fill two pieces of bread. This is perfect, of course, if you have two dogs. Or, cover remaining egg and refrigerate to use another day. Better yet, fix a piece of Bone-ifried Bread for yourself or your child to have for breakfast while your dog is enjoying his breakfast.

This 1950s favorite is comfort food for dogs, just as it is for their people.

INGREDIENTS

1 cup (240 g) Westie White Sauce (page 54)

2½ cups (375 g) medium egg noodles, cooked and drained

One 6-ounce (170 g) can tuna, drained

½ cup (75 g) frozen peas

TUNA NOODLE CASSEROLE

DIRECTIONS

1 Place all ingredients in a medium bowl and mix thoroughly to combine.

2 Spoon into muffin cups and bake in a preheated 400°F (200°C) oven about 15 minutes.

3 Remove from oven and let cool in pan about 15 minutes. Remove individual casseroles from pan. Makes 12 casseroles.

NOTE: Once cooled, individual casseroles may be wrapped in plastic and kept refrigerated. When ready to serve, microwave one casserole 30 to 45 seconds.

*This classic combination
has proven pooch appeal.*

MAC 'N' CHEESE WITH SAUSAGE

INGREDIENTS

1 cup (240 g) Four Cheese Sauce (page 57)

¼ pound (115 g) mild sausage, cut into bite-sized pieces and cooked

2 cups (300 g) elbow macaroni, cooked and drained

DIRECTIONS

1 Place all ingredients in a medium bowl and mix thoroughly to combine.

2 Spoon into muffin cups and bake in a preheated 400°F (200°C) oven about 15 minutes.

3 Remove from oven and let cool in pan about 15 minutes. Remove individual casseroles from pan. Makes 12 casseroles.

NOTE: Once cooled, individual casseroles may be wrapped in plastic and kept refrigerated. When ready to serve, microwave one casserole 30 to 45 seconds.

As all-American and indeterminate in origin as any mixed-breed dog, meatloaf is a dinnertime favorite that pooches are advised to share with their people.

GIVE-A-DOG-A-BONE MEATLOAF

INGREDIENTS

¾ cup (170 ml) water

1 carrot, peeled and diced

1 celery stalk, diced

1¾ pounds (790 g) meatloaf mix*

1 cup (100 g) old-fashioned oatmeal

1 egg, slightly beaten

1 tablespoon ketchup

*A combination of ground beef, ground pork, and ground veal (or chicken or turkey).

DIRECTIONS

1 Bring water to boil in a small skillet. Add carrot and celery. Reduce heat to medium and cook 5 minutes. Drain and let cool slightly.

2 Place all ingredients in a large bowl and mix thoroughly to combine.

3 Place meatloaf on foil-lined baking sheet. Form into a bone shape measuring approximately 9 inches (22.5 cm) long by 5 inches (12.5 cm) wide by 1½ inches (4 cm) high. Bake in a preheated 350°F (180°C) oven about 1 hour.

4 Remove from oven and let cool about 10 minutes. If desired, spread additional ketchup or mild barbecue sauce on top of meatloaf, pipe mashed potatoes around the lower edge, and garnish with a cheese slice cutout. Makes 1 meatloaf.

*Dogs don't mind leftovers,
especially when formed into croquettes
and cooked just for them.*

TURKEY CROQUETTES

DIRECTIONS

1 Place turkey, wheat germ, egg, white sauce, and peas in a medium bowl and mix thoroughly to combine. Refrigerate 2 hours.

2 Roll turkey mixture into 1-inch (2.5 cm) balls. Flatten slightly and coat in bread crumbs.

3 Heat oil in small skillet over medium heat. Place about half the croquettes in the hot oil and cook until light brown on each side, about 1 to 2 minutes. Makes 18 to 20 croquettes. Serve with cooked rice.

NOTE: Croquettes can be prepared up to several days in advance. Simply follow directions to step 2, cover croquettes with plastic wrap, and keep refrigerated. Cook as needed.

INGREDIENTS

1 cup (125 g) cooked turkey, coarsely ground

½ cup (50 g) wheat germ

1 egg, slightly beaten

1 tablespoon Westie White Sauce (page 54)

1 tablespoon frozen peas

¼ cup (30 g) plain dry bread crumbs

⅓ cup (80 ml) vegetable oil

Cooked rice

Terriers are particularly fond of mice and other vermin, so this dish was created with terriers' favorite prey in mind.

MICE ON RICE

DIRECTIONS

1 Place chicken, oatmeal, carrot, and egg in a large bowl and mix thoroughly to combine.

2 Place meat mixture on a foil-lined baking sheet and pat into a ½-inch- (13 mm) thick rectangle. Bake in a preheated 375°F (190°C) oven for 30 minutes.

3 Remove from oven and let loaf rest for at least 15 minutes. Using a mouse-shaped cookie cutter, cut loaf into mice. **

4 To serve, sprinkle cooked rice over dry dog food and place one or more mice on top of the rice. Makes approximately 12 mice, plus scraps.

**Or, use other cookie cutters to cut into your dog's favorite prey or a bone shape. Or, simply cut into bite-sized pieces.

INGREDIENTS

1 pound (450 g) ground chicken or turkey

1 cup (100 g) old-fashioned oatmeal*

1½ cups (180 g) grated carrot

1 egg

Cooked rice

*Or, use 2 slices bread, soaked in water and pressed dry.

CHAPTER 3

GRAVIES AND SAUCES

As a change of pace from stew, gravies and sauces make a tantalizing topping to your dog's dry dog food. Gravies and sauces add flavor and tweak the appetite of even the most jaded dog. All are easy to make, and most take advantage of leftovers and make enough to last from several days to a week, depending on the size of your dog. They can be poured over dry dog food and called a meal. Or, add tidbits of meat, vegetables, rice, or potatoes for even more appetite appeal.

Southern to the bone, red-eye gravy is made from ham drippings. Serve with grits and biscuits to get the total Southern experience.

RED-EYE GRAVY WITH GRITS, HAM, AND BISCUITS

INGREDIENTS

2½ cups (300 g) all-purpose baking mix

⅔ cup (150 ml) milk

¼ pound (115 g) ham steak, ¼ inch (6 mm) thick, cut into bite-sized pieces

1 cup (225 ml) water

1 cup (240 g) prepared grits

DIRECTIONS

1 Place baking mix and milk in medium bowl. Mix and roll out according to package directions. Using a cookie cutter, cut into bone shapes. Place biscuits on ungreased cookie sheet and bake in a preheated 450°F (230°C) oven for 8 to 10 minutes until golden brown. Set aside.

2 Meanwhile, in small skillet over medium heat, cook ham, stirring occasionally, until ham is browned and warm, about 4 to 5 minutes. Remove ham from pan. Set aside.

3 Add ½ cup (115 ml) water to skillet and stir to loosen any brown bits. Add remaining water and cook until gravy starts to boil, about 1 to 2 minutes. Makes about ½ cup (115 ml).

4 To serve, stir about 1 tablespoon gravy into dry dog food. Top with about ¼ cup (60 g) grits. Make a well in center of grits and fill with additional gravy. Add a few pieces of ham alongside the grits and place one or two bone-shaped biscuits on top.

Bone Up on Your People Skills

Listen up, pup! You're new here, so there's a lot you don't know yet. Success in this doggone business all comes down to one thing: people-management skills. I am going to let you in on all the things I have learned about people, so you, too, will grow up to be a Lucky Dog.

1 First off, there's the whole business of where to do your business. The answer is always: OUTSIDE! The sooner you get the idea, the better. Once you master that, you pretty much can do whatever else you please.

2 It's a good sign that your person bought this book. I suggest you look through it and put your dirty paw print on all the recipes you want her to fix.

3 Some people act like they own you. No, you own them. Try to get someone who works from home so you can go in or out whenever you please. If you have a person who leaves every day to go to work, whatever that is, then here's what I suggest:

a Lie there and look really sad. It makes them feel guilty. This is very good because then they give you treats (see chapters 4 and 5).

b Or, stand at the front window (you little guys may have to stand up on the back of the couch) and bark as loudly as possible until you can't see the car anymore. Then you can go back to napping. That way, they will be worried about you all day and maybe will even come home for lunch. (See chapters 4 and 5 on treats, again.)

Anytime you roast a chicken or turkey, save those giblets that the rest of the family doesn't want. Whether you use them right away or freeze them for a later date, your dog will always appreciate a little giblet gravy with his dinner.

GIBLET GRAVY

INGREDIENTS

2 tablespoons vegetable oil

½ pound (115 g) chicken or turkey giblets

2 tablespoons all-purpose flour

1 cup (225 ml) chicken broth

DIRECTIONS

1 Heat oil in small skillet over medium heat. Add giblets and cook, stirring frequently, until giblets are thoroughly cooked, about 5 minutes.

2 With slotted spoon, remove giblets from pan. Cut into bite-sized pieces or, if preferred, purée in blender with chicken broth.

3 Add flour to skillet and stir to combine with oil in pan to form a paste. Slowly add chicken broth, stirring constantly to stir up any brown bits in pan and incorporate flour mixture until smooth.

4 Return giblets to pan and stir 1 to 2 minutes until gravy comes to a boil and thickens slightly. Makes about 1 cup (225 ml).

4 Pick a favorite chair or couch to sleep on. Even if your person tells you to get down, just get right back up on it. Pretty soon your person will get the idea and cover it with an old blanket and then you own it, baby.

5 Make friends with any kids or grandkids in the house. They are lower to the ground and they are always eating something. It's easy to get them to share food with you.

6 If you're having a good time playing outside and someone tells you to "come," pretend to be deaf—unless, of course, it's suppertime.

7 Make sure you get the best spot for watching TV at night. The middle of the couch is perfect. Then your people can sit next to you. An ottoman is always good, too, or, if you're really lucky, the recliner.

8 Assure your people that you will always keep their feet warm at night if they just let you up on the bed. Then hog all the covers.

Remember, it's a dog's life. Live it well.

Poured over even the poorest dry dog food, this sauce will leave your dog licking his lips, and the bowl. Save some sauce, though, to make Liver Lips (page 75).

LIP-LICKIN' LIVER-LOVER'S SAUCE

DIRECTIONS

1 Heat oil in skillet over medium-high heat. Add chicken livers and cook, stirring frequently, until livers are brown, about 5 to 6 minutes.

2 Place cooked livers, including oil, in blender with chicken broth and purée until smooth. Makes about 3 cups (675 ml).

INGREDIENTS

2 tablespoons vegetable oil

1 pound (450 g) chicken livers

2 cups (450 ml) chicken broth

Any West Highland White Terrier, or Bichon Frise, or white Poodle, will tell you that white works with everything, and such is the case with this versatile sauce.

WESTIE WHITE SAUCE

DIRECTIONS

1 Melt butter in medium saucepan over medium heat.

2 Add flour, a little at a time, stirring constantly until all flour has been incorporated. Cook and stir an additional 2 to 3 minutes.

3 Slowly add milk, stirring constantly, until sauce is thick and smooth but does not boil, about 18 to 20 minutes.

4 Pour sauce into airtight plastic container. Place plastic wrap directly on sauce to prevent "skin" from forming. Let cool and refrigerate. Makes about 1 quart (0.95 L).

INGREDIENTS

½ cup (1 stick; 115 g) butter or margarine

½ cup (60 g) all-purpose flour

1 quart (0.95 L) milk

It sounds gourmet, but don't wait for a special occasion to serve it to your dog.

BEEF STROGANOFF SAUCE

DIRECTIONS

1 Heat oil in small skillet over medium-high heat. Add cube steak and mushrooms and cook, stirring frequently, about 2 to 3 minutes.

2 Add white sauce and cook, stirring constantly, just until warm, about 1 minute. Makes about 1½ cups (360 g).

3 To serve, stir plain yogurt into sauce just before ladling over or stirring into dry dog food. Garnish with chopped parsley, if desired.

INGREDIENTS

1 tablespoon vegetable oil

¼ pound (115 g) cube steak, cut into bite-sized pieces

¼ cup (50 g) sliced mushrooms

1 cup (240 g) Westie White Sauce (page 54)

1 teaspoon to 1 tablespoon plain yogurt

Other Tempting Toppers

Any of the sauces and gravies in this chapter make delectable toppings for ordinary dry dog food. If your dog is a fussy eater or just bored with plain dry dog food, try one of these easy ideas for enhancing his appetite:

- Grated or crumbled cheese

- Shredded carrots

- Peanut butter

- Leftover gravy

- Plain yogurt, on its own or mixed with peanut butter, honey, or pumpkin purée

- Cottage cheese

- Leftover beef, chicken, or other meat

The King Charles spaniel might find this humble but tasty sauce somewhat plebeian for his aristocratic palate, but he would probably lap it up when you weren't looking.

INGREDIENTS

1 teaspoon olive oil

¼ cup (25 g) chopped mushrooms

1 cup (125 g) cooked chopped chicken or turkey

¼ cup (38 g) frozen peas

1 cup (240 g) Westie White Sauce (page 54)

CHICKEN-A-LA-KING SAUCE

DIRECTIONS

1 Heat oil in small saucepan over medium heat. Add mushrooms, cooking and stirring, 1 to 2 minutes.

2 Add chicken and peas. Cook and stir an additional 30 seconds.

3 Add white sauce and cook, stirring constantly, until sauce is warm, about 1 minute. Makes about 2½ cups (600 g).

Dogs love cheese, from plain ol' American to the finest French types. Use four of your dog's favorite cheeses, or whatever is left over in the refrigerator, to make this cheese-licious sauce.

INGREDIENTS

1 cup (240 g) Westie White Sauce (page 54)

¼ cup (30 g) cheddar cheese, shredded

¼ cup (30 g) swiss cheese, shredded

¼ cup (30 g) mozzarella cheese, shredded

¼ cup (30 g) blue cheese, crumbled

FOUR CHEESE SAUCE

DIRECTIONS

1 Place white sauce in small saucepan over medium heat and cook, stirring constantly, until warm but not boiling.

2 Add cheeses and cook, stirring frequently, until melted. Makes about 1½ cups (360 g).

This casual favorite is easy to make.

TUNA MELT

DIRECTIONS
Place cheese sauce and tuna in small saucepan over medium heat and cook, stirring constantly, until warm but not boiling, about 3 to 4 minutes. Makes about 1½ cups (360 g).

INGREDIENTS

1 cup (240 g) Four Cheese Sauce (page 57)

One 6-ounce (170 g) can tuna, drained

CHAPTER 4

SAVORY SNACKS

Offer your dog one of these homemade meaty morsels and he may "sit" or "stay" on command. Or, he may just come running to get his teeth into one of these flavorful cookies. Whether you use them as bait in the show ring, as a reward on the agility course or in obedience training, or just as a treat because your dog is so darn cute and lovable, making these savory snacks will be its own reward. Cut them into bone shapes, other cute shapes as suggested here, or just bite-sized strips. Your dog won't care as long as he gets one as soon as it comes out of the oven.

Baked with real beef, these cookies will have your dog barking and begging for more.

BEEF BARLEY BONES

INGREDIENTS

¼ cup (60 ml) vegetable oil

¼ pound (115 g) ground beef

1 cup (225 ml) beef broth

4 cups (500 g) whole wheat flour

2 cups (310 g) cooked barley

4 tablespoons dried oregano

2 tablespoons Worcestershire sauce

DIRECTIONS

1 Heat vegetable oil in skillet over medium-high heat. Add ground beef and cook, stirring frequently, until meat is brown, about 3 to 4 minutes.

2 Place cooked beef, including oil, in blender with beef broth. Purée.

3 Place flour, cooked barley, beef purée, oregano, and Worcestershire sauce in large bowl. Mix thoroughly to combine.

4 Roll out dough on floured surface to about ¼-inch (6 mm) thick. Using a cookie cutter, cut into bone shapes. Combine dough scraps and continue to roll out and cut into shapes until all dough has been used.

5 Place cookies on ungreased foil-lined baking sheets, and bake in a preheated 325°F (170°C) oven for 30 to 35 minutes. Turn off oven and let cookies dry in oven for 3 hours or overnight. Makes 5 to 6 dozen cookies.

The Low-Down on Dog Cookie Dough

These cookie doughs are all very stiff. They can be mixed easily in a heavy-duty stand mixer using the paddle attachment. Or, mix them with your hands to incorporate all ingredients. Wear plastic foodservice gloves if you wish.

About Baking and Storing Cookies

■ Cookies can be placed close together on a baking sheet because they do not rise or spread.

■ Four baking sheets should be able to accommodate all the cookies. They can be baked in the oven all at once by placing two baking sheets on a rack positioned in the top third of the oven and two baking sheets on a rack positioned in the bottom third of the oven.

■ If you notice that cookies in the bottom third of the oven, or cookies at the back, are baking faster than the ones in the top third, or in the front of the oven, switch positions or rotate about halfway through the cooking process.

■ Once cooled, store cookies in an airtight container or zipper-style plastic bag at room temperature. They should keep for at least 3 months.

■ Unused savory doughs can be kept overnight in the refrigerator. Bake the next day. Or, freeze dough, then thaw in the refrigerator and bake according to recipe directions at a more convenient time.

■ Unused sweet doughs can be kept several days in the refrigerator. Or, freeze dough, then thaw in the refrigerator and bake according to recipe directions at a more convenient time.

*Your dog won't need to go to school
to know he loves these salmony,
fish-shaped cookies.*

SOMETHING FISHY

INGREDIENTS

4 cups (500 g) whole wheat flour

2 cups (420 g) mashed potatoes

1 cup (225 ml) chicken broth

One 6-ounce (170 g) can skinless, boneless
salmon, drained

4 tablespoons dried dill weed

¼ cup (60 ml) olive oil

DIRECTIONS

1 Place all ingredients in a large bowl. Mix thoroughly to combine.

2 Roll out dough on floured surface to about ¼-inch (6 mm) thick. Using a cookie cutter, cut into fish shapes. Combine dough scraps and continue to roll out and cut into shapes until all dough has been used.

3 Place cookies on ungreased foil-lined baking sheets, and bake in a preheated 325°F (170°C) oven for 30 to 35 minutes. Turn off oven and let cookies dry in oven for 3 hours or overnight. Makes 5 to 6 dozen cookies.

Whether you have a tea party for your fur-friends or just want to offer a midafternoon snack, these sandwich squares also make a great way to disguise a dreaded pill.

INGREDIENTS

4 cups (500 g) whole wheat flour

2 cups (250 g) all-purpose flour

One 14½-ounce (429 ml) can chicken broth

4 tablespoons dried parsley flakes

2 tablespoons vegetable oil

DoggieWiches

DIRECTIONS

1 Place all ingredients in a large bowl. Mix thoroughly to combine.

2 Roll out dough on floured surface to about ⅛-inch (3 mm) thick and cut into squares using a cookie cutter. Combine dough scraps and continue to roll out and cut into shapes until all dough has been used.

3 Place cookies on ungreased foil-lined baking sheets, and bake in a preheated 325°F (170°C) oven for 30 to 35 minutes. Turn off oven and let cookies dry in oven for 3 hours or overnight. Place dog's favorite sandwich filling (such as peanut butter or ham and cheese) between two squares. Makes 5 to 6 dozen sandwich cookies.

Don't wait for Valentine's Day to make these heart-shaped, heart-filled cookies.

HOUND HEARTS

DIRECTIONS

1 Heat vegetable oil in skillet over medium-high heat. Add chicken hearts and cook, stirring frequently, until brown, about 3 to 4 minutes.

2 Place cooked chicken hearts, including oil, in blender with tomatoes, including juice. Purée.

3 Place flour, cooked rice, chicken-heart purée, and basil in a large bowl. Mix thoroughly to combine.

4 Roll out dough on floured surface to about ¼-inch (6 mm) thick. Using a cookie cutter, cut into heart shapes. Combine dough scraps and continue to roll out and cut into shapes until all dough has been used.

5 Place cookies on ungreased foil-lined baking sheets, and bake in a preheated 325°F (170°C) oven for 30 to 35 minutes. Turn off oven and let cookies dry in oven for 3 hours or overnight. Makes 5 to 6 dozen cookies

INGREDIENTS

¼ cup (60 ml) vegetable oil

¼ pound (115 g) chicken hearts (or combination of hearts and gizzards)

One 14½-ounce (429 ml) can diced tomatoes in juice

4 cups (500 g) whole wheat flour

2 cups (330 g) cooked rice

4 tablespoons dried basil

DOGGEREL

Be my canine Valentine. I make these Hound Hearts for all the dogs I love, package a dozen or so in a cute box, and deliver them with a card from "a secret admirer."

This snack has all the delicious taste of Sunday chicken dinner baked right into a dog cookie.

INGREDIENTS

¼ cup (60 ml) vegetable oil

¼ pound (115 g) ground or minced chicken

¼ cup (30 g) minced celery

1 cup (225 ml) chicken broth

4 cups (500 g) whole wheat flour

2 cups (330 g) cooked rice

4 tablespoons dried sage

DIRECTIONS

1 Heat vegetable oil in skillet over medium-high heat. Add ground chicken and celery and cook, stirring frequently, until meat is no longer pink, about 3 to 4 minutes.

2 Place cooked chicken and celery, including oil, in blender with chicken broth. Purée.

3 Combine flour, cooked rice, chicken purée, and sage in a large bowl. Mix thoroughly to combine.

4 Roll out dough on floured surface to about ¼-inch (6 mm) thick. Using a cookie cutter, cut into bone shapes. Combine dough scraps and continue to roll out and cut into shapes until all dough has been used.

5 Place cookies on ungreased foil-lined baking sheets, and bake in a preheated 325°F (170°C) oven for 30 to 35 minutes. Turn off oven and let cookies dry in oven for 3 hours or overnight. Makes about 5 to 6 dozen cookies.

Other Okay Snacks

- Apple slices
- Baby carrots
- Plain popcorn
- Romaine lettuce ribs
- Salt-free pretzels

*Your dog might do a jiggedy-jig
when he bites into these plump piggy tidbits.*

LI'L PORKERS

INGREDIENTS

¼ cup (60 ml) vegetable oil

4 ounces (115 g) ground pork

One 14½-ounce (429 ml) can chicken broth

4 cups (500 g) whole wheat flour

2 cups (420 g) mashed potatoes

¼ cup (30 g) shredded carrot

¼ cup (38 g) minced apple

4 tablespoons ground rosemary

DIRECTIONS

1 Heat vegetable oil in skillet over medium-high heat. Add ground pork and cook, stirring frequently, until meat is no longer pink, about 3 to 4 minutes.

2 Place cooked pork, including oil, in blender with chicken broth. Purée.

3 Place flour, mashed potatoes, pork purée, carrot, apple, and rosemary in a large bowl. Mix thoroughly to combine.

4 Roll out dough on floured surface to about ¼-inch (6 mm) thick. Using a cookie cutter, cut into piggy shapes. Combine dough scraps and continue to roll out and cut into shapes until all dough has been used. With a toothpick, make an eye and smile on the piggy faces, if desired.

5 Place cookies on ungreased foil-lined baking sheets, and bake in a preheated 325°F (170°C) oven for 30 to 35 minutes. Turn off oven and let cookies dry in oven for 3 hours or overnight. Makes 5 to 6 dozen cookies.

These snacks will bring a smile to your, and your dog's, face.

LIVER LIPS

INGREDIENTS

4 cups (500 g) whole wheat flour

2 cups (420 g) mashed potatoes

1½ cups (340 ml) Lip-Lickin' Liver-Lover's Sauce (page 54)

4 tablespoons dried thyme

2 tablespoons Dijon-style mustard

DIRECTIONS

1 Place all ingredients in a large bowl. Mix thoroughly to combine.

2 Roll out dough on floured surface to about ¼-inch (6 mm) thick. Using a cookie cutter, cut into lip shapes. With the point of a knife, make a line through lips to form a partial smile. Combine dough scraps and continue to roll out and cut into shapes until all dough has been used.

3 Place cookies on ungreased foil-lined baking sheets, and bake in a preheated 325°F (170°C) oven for 30 to 35 minutes. Turn off oven and let cookies dry in oven for 3 hours or overnight. Makes about 5 to 6 dozen cookies.

*Curl up on the couch with your pooch,
pop* Lady and the Tramp *into the DVD player, and offer
a slice or two of Poochie Pizza for a snack.*

POOCHIE PIZZAS

DIRECTIONS

1 Place all ingredients in a large bowl.
Mix thoroughly to combine.

2 Roll out dough on floured surface to about
¼-inch (6 mm) thick. Using a round cookie
or biscuit cutter, cut into circles. Then cut each
circle into 4 wedges as if slicing a pizza. Crimp
rounded end of each wedge to resemble a pizza
crust. Combine dough scraps and continue to
roll out and cut into shapes until all dough has
been used.

3 Place cookies on ungreased foil-lined baking
sheets, and bake in a preheated 325°F (170°C)
oven for 30 to 35 minutes. Turn off oven and
let cookies dry in oven for 3 hours or overnight.
While cookies are still slightly warm, sprinkle
with additional shredded mozzarella, if desired.
Makes 5 to 6 dozen cookies.

INGREDIENTS

4 cups (500 g) whole wheat flour

2 cups (330 g) cooked orzo

One 14½-ounce (429 ml) can diced tomatoes in
juice

¼ pound (115 g) mild Italian sausage, minced,
cooked, and drained on paper towels

4 tablespoons pizza seasoning*

¼ cup (60 ml) olive oil

2 tablespoons shredded mozzarella

*Or make your own pizza seasoning from 2 tablespoons ground
fennel seed, 1 tablespoon dried oregano, and 1 tablespoon
dried basil.

CHAPTER 5

SWEET TREATS

When you eat cookies, you find it hard to resist that longing gaze, that cocked head, that wagging tail.

Don't deny your dog the occasional sweet treat. Bake him his very own cookies. Made with whole wheat flour and other grains, these cookies disguise their doggone goodness with the peanut butter, pumpkin, applesauce, and other appetizing ingredients that appeal to your dog's sweet tooth.

There is probably no dog on the planet that doesn't love the flavor of peanut butter. If you make no other cookie, make this one.

INGREDIENTS

4 cups (500 g) whole wheat flour

2 cups (200 g) wheat germ

2 cups (450 g) peanut butter

1½ cups (340 ml) water

¼ cup (90 g) honey

¼ cup (30 g) ground peanuts

PEANUT BUTTER BONES

DIRECTIONS

1   Place all ingredients in a large bowl. Mix thoroughly to combine.

2   Roll out dough on floured surface to about ¼-inch (6 mm) thick. Using a cookie cutter, cut into bone shapes. Combine dough scraps and continue to roll out and cut into shapes until all dough has been used.

3   Place cookies on ungreased foil-lined baking sheets, and bake in a preheated 325°F (170°C) oven for 30 to 35 minutes. Makes 5 to 6 dozen cookies.

Dogs love the taste and aroma of their very own gingery cookie.

INGREDIENTS

4 cups (500 g) all-purpose flour

2 cups (250 g) whole wheat flour

1 cup (350 g) molasses

1 cup (225 ml) water

½ cup (120 ml) vegetable oil

4 tablespoons ground ginger

2 teaspoons ground cinnamon

1 teaspoon ground cloves

GINGERBONES

DIRECTIONS

1 Place all ingredients in a large bowl. Mix thoroughly to combine.

2 Roll out dough on floured surface to about ¼-inch (6 mm) thick. Using a cookie cutter, cut into bone shapes. Combine dough scraps and continue to roll out and cut into shapes until all dough has been used.

3 Place cookies on ungreased foil-lined baking sheets, and bake in a preheated 325°F (170°C) oven for 30 to 35 minutes. Makes 5 to 6 dozen cookies.

This is a classic cookie for a classy dog.

SnickerPoodles

DIRECTIONS

1 Place all ingredients in a large bowl. Mix thoroughly to combine.

2 Roll out dough on floured surface to about ¼-inch (6 mm) thick. Using a cookie cutter, cut into poodle shapes. Combine dough scraps and continue to roll out and cut into shapes until all dough has been used.

3 Place cookies on ungreased foil-lined baking sheets, and bake in a preheated 325°F (170°C) oven for 30 to 35 minutes. Makes 5 to 6 dozen cookies.

INGREDIENTS

5 cups (625 g) all-purpose flour

One 25-ounce (739 ml) jar applesauce

2 cups (200 g) old-fashioned oatmeal

4 tablespoons ground cinnamon

2 tablespoons vegetable oil

2 tablespoons honey

TIP

Measure vegetable oil first; then use the same measuring spoon to measure the honey, and it will slide out slickly. Use this same technique with other sticky ingredients such as molasses.

*Everyone's favorite cake gets turned into
every dog's favorite cookie.*

INGREDIENTS

4 cups (500 g) whole wheat flour

2 cups (200 g) wheat germ

1½ cups (340 g) mashed cooked carrots

1 cup (225 ml) water

One 8-ounce (237 ml) can crushed pineapple
with juice

4 tablespoons ground nutmeg

2 tablespoons vegetable oil

2 tablespoons honey

CARROT CAKE COOKIES

DIRECTIONS

1 Place all ingredients in a large bowl. Mix thoroughly to combine.

2 Roll out dough on floured surface to about ¼-inch (6 mm) thick.
Using a cookie cutter, cut into rounds. Combine dough scraps
and continue to roll out and cut into shapes until all dough has
been used.

3 Place cookies on ungreased foil-lined baking sheets, and bake in
a preheated 325°F (170°C) oven for 30 to 35 minutes.
Makes 5 to 6 dozen cookies.

*These treats will make your dog
sit up and say, "Bow Wow."*

BANANA BONES

INGREDIENTS

4 cups (500 g) whole wheat flour

2 cups (230 g) Grape-Nuts cereal

2 cups (600 g) mashed banana (about 5)

¾ cup (170 ml) water

4 tablespoons ground nutmeg

2 tablespoons vegetable oil

2 tablespoons honey

DIRECTIONS

1 Place all ingredients in a large bowl.
   Mix thoroughly to combine.

2 Roll out dough on floured surface to about
   ¼-inch (6 mm) thick. Using a cookie cutter,
   cut into bone shapes. Combine dough scraps
   and continue to roll out and cut into shapes
   until all dough has been used.

3 Place cookies on ungreased foil-lined baking
   sheets, and bake in a preheated 325°F
   (170°C) oven for 30 to 35 minutes. Makes 5
   to 6 dozen cookies.

In addition to peanut butter, pumpkin is one of dog's favorite flavors. Offer these treats at Halloween, Thanksgiving, Christmas, or any time of year.

PUMPKIN PUPPERS

DIRECTIONS

1 Place all ingredients in a large bowl. Mix thoroughly to combine.

2 Roll out dough on floured surface to about ¼-inch (6 mm) thick. Using a cookie cutter, cut into doggie shapes. Combine dough scraps and continue to roll out and cut into shapes until all dough has been used.

3 Place cookies on ungreased foil-lined baking sheets, and bake in a preheated 325°F (170°C) oven for 30 to 35 minutes. Makes 5 to 6 dozen cookies.

INGREDIENTS

4 cups (500 g) whole wheat flour

2 cups (200 g) wheat germ

One 15-ounce (426 g) can pumpkin

1 cup (225 ml) water

4 tablespoons pumpkin pie spice

2 tablespoons vegetable oil

2 tablespoons honey

The goodness of oatmeal and apple get together in one outstanding cookie.

OATMEAL-APPLE COOKIES

DIRECTIONS

1 Place all ingredients in a large bowl. Mix thoroughly to combine.

2 Roll out dough on floured surface to about ¼-inch (6 mm) thick. Using a cookie cutter, cut into bone shapes. Combine dough scraps and continue to roll out and cut into shapes until all dough has been used.

3 Place cookies on ungreased foil-lined baking sheets, and bake in a preheated 325°F (170°C) oven for 30 to 35 minutes. Makes 5 to 6 dozen cookies

INGREDIENTS

4 cups (500 g) whole wheat flour

2 cups (200 g) old-fashioned oatmeal

1¼ cups (280 ml) water

¼ cup (38 g) minced apple

3 tablespoons ground cinnamon

2 tablespoons vegetable oil

2 tablespoons honey

1 tablespoon ground cloves

Lots of great grains plus the subtle sweetness of Chinese five-spice powder will extinguish midafternoon hunger pangs.

MULTIGRAIN FIVE-SPICE FIRE HYDRANTS

INGREDIENTS

4 cups (500 g) whole wheat flour

2 cups (330 g) cooked brown rice

2 cups (450 ml) water

¾ cup (85 g) Grape-Nuts cereal

¾ cup (75 g) old-fashioned oatmeal

½ cup (50 g) wheat germ

4 tablespoons Chinese five-spice powder

2 tablespoons vegetable oil

2 tablespoons honey

DIRECTIONS

1 Place all ingredients in a large bowl. Mix thoroughly to combine.

2 Roll out dough on floured surface to about ¼-inch (6 mm) thick. Using a cookie cutter, cut into fire hydrant shapes. Combine dough scraps and continue to roll out and cut into shapes until all dough has been used.

3 Place cookies on ungreased foil-lined baking sheets, and bake in a preheated 325°F (170°C) oven for 30 to 35 minutes. Makes 5 to 6 dozen cookies.

CHAPTER 6

PARTY AND HOLIDAY FOOD

Let's face it, dogs are party animals. Your birthday or theirs, they may join in the singing. At Halloween, they tolerantly submit to wearing a costume so they can go trick-or-treating with the kids (no chocolate, though!). At Thanksgiving, they will want to see turkey and mashed potatoes in their bowl. And pooches of all persuasions will happily partake of Passover, Christmas, and Kwanzaa feasts.

This recipe rated a twenty-dog pack paw of approval after being served at one lucky Lab's birthday party.

BOWZER'S BIRTHDAY CAKE

INGREDIENTS

1 pound (450 g) ground turkey or chicken

2 carrots, diced

One 10-ounce (284 g) package frozen spinach, thawed and squeezed dry

1 cup (165 g) cooked brown rice

1 tablespoon vegetable oil

1 egg, slightly beaten

2 hard-cooked eggs, sliced

DIRECTIONS

1 Place turkey, carrots, spinach, brown rice, oil, and raw egg in a large bowl. Mix thoroughly to combine.

2 Pat half the mixture into a greased and waxed-paper-lined 9-inch (22.5 cm) cake pan.

3 Layer hard-cooked egg slices over mixture, then top with remaining meat mixture. Bake in a preheated 350°F (180°C) oven for 45 to 50 minutes or until done.

4 Remove from oven and let rest in pan for 5 minutes. Using a large spatula, remove from pan, draining off any grease, and allow to cool on platter for 15 minutes before frosting and serving. Makes 1 cake layer.

NOTE: To make a layer cake, double recipe and use two 9-inch (22.5 cm) cake pans. When cake layers are baked and cooled, place one layer on plate. Spread with about 2 cups (420 g) mashed potatoes, then place other cake layer on top of mashed potato filling. Using a pastry bag with a large star tip, make mashed potato rosettes for candles, if desired.

DOGGEREL

This recipe was adapted from one provided by Suzanne, the human organizer of a dog playgroup that meets informally every Sunday to cavort in a nearby park. All comers are welcome. Suzanne has made the cake on the previous page in a single layer and frosted it with soy-based "cream cheese" for her dog Gabriella's birthday. She has also put the meat mixture, with just one egg slice in the center, into muffin cups and frosted it with mashed potatoes for Buddy's party. You could also form the loaf into a large bone shape to be shared by all dogs at the party or into individual bone shapes.

Suzanne's Tips for Throwing a Dog Birthday Party

➤ Make sure all the dogs get along.

➤ Have the birthday party in an area large enough to accommodate all the guests. Limit guest list to four or five dogs if it is an indoor party. Invite up to twenty if the party is held outdoors, either in your own backyard or a dog-friendly park.

➤ Bring water and bowls for the dogs.

➤ Keep paper towels nearby for pick-up.

➤ Hold the party in the morning when dogs are lively and no one is too grouchy.

➤ Bring sturdy paper plates to serve each dog a piece of birthday cake.

➤ Have food and beverages available for the people, too.

➤ Dress up the dogs. While most dogs will not willingly wear party hats—heck, even kids don't like those—dogs will wear scarves. You may want to go to the fabric store and purchase a length of material that you cut into bandanna-sized scarves with pinking shears so all the party dogs have something to wear.

Play games:

DRY DOG FOOD TOSS—The people stand about five feet (1.5 m) away and toss pieces of dry dog food to their dogs. Whichever dog catches the most dry dog food, wins.

KISSIE—Get all dogs in a line while people stand about twenty feet (6.1 m) away. People call their dogs, and whichever dog comes first and gives kisses, wins.

STICK—People throw sticks for their dogs. Whichever dog brings back the stick first, wins.

OBSTACLE COURSE—Create a for-fun-only obstacle course with hula hoops, toilet plungers, or cloth-draped tables. Of course, people may have to go first to show their dogs how to run the course.

➤ Award prizes to everyone. Go to a dollar store, craft store, or pet store and buy inexpensive items such as tennis balls, rubber balls, bones, rope toys, or other playthings for prizes. Every dog should go home a winner.

Whether your canine keeps kosher or not, he will still appreciate matzos over chicken broth.

ROVER'S PASSOVER MATZOS

INGREDIENTS

1 matzo

1 cup cold water

1 tablespoon vegetable oil

½ teaspoon dried parsley flakes

1 egg, slightly beaten

2 tablespoons ground matzo meal

4 quarts (3.8 L) water

DIRECTIONS

1 Soak matzo in 1 cup cold water for about 5 minutes. Press dry.

2 Place soaked matzo, oil, parsley flakes, egg, and matzo meal in a small bowl. Mix thoroughly to combine. Chill for at least 1 hour.

3 Wet hands and roll matzo mixture into bite-sized balls.

4 Meanwhile, bring 4 quarts (3.8 L) water to a full rolling boil in a large saucepan over high heat. Drop balls into water and cook for about 20 minutes. Makes about 16 balls.

5 To serve, ladle chicken broth over dry dog food and add one or more matzo balls.

What's scarier than a cat at Halloween?
This cat is one your dog will enjoy catching.

CREEPY CAT CAKE

INGREDIENTS

1 cup (125 g) whole wheat flour

1 cup (100 g) old-fashioned oatmeal

1 teaspoon baking powder

1 teaspoon pumpkin pie spice

½ cup (115 g) canned pumpkin

¼ cup (90 g) honey

1 egg, slightly beaten

2 tablespoons water

2 tablespoons chopped walnuts

2 tablespoons raisins (optional)

DIRECTIONS

1 Place flour, oatmeal, baking powder, and pumpkin pie spice in a medium bowl and mix to combine. Make a well in the center.

2 In a separate bowl, stir together pumpkin, honey, egg, and water.

3 Pour pumpkin mixture into flour mixture and stir for 4 to 5 strokes. Add walnuts and raisins and stir just to combine all ingredients.

4 Spray inside of large cat mold and parchment paper with cooking oil. Place cat mold on parchment-lined cookie sheet. Spoon pumpkin mixture into the mold to within ¼ inch (6 mm) of the top. Remaining batter can be spooned into greased muffin cups and baked alongside the cat. Bake in a preheated 400°F (200°C) oven for 20 minutes. Remove from oven and let cool in mold for 5 minutes. Remove from mold and continue cooling on rack. Makes 1 cat cake and about 3 or 4 muffins.

A Word about Raisins

Recent reports indicate that some dogs have suffered kidney failure after eating large quantities of green grapes or raisins. If a dog has a toxic reaction to grapes or raisins, he will have vomiting and/or diarrhea within twenty-four hours. Of course, he should be seen by a vet immediately.

The ASPCA notes that veterinary toxicologists at the Animal Poison Control Center are investigating these reports because it is unclear what the exact role grapes or raisins may have played in these cases.

Dogs love the sweetness and chewy texture of raisins, and raisins have been kept to a minimum in this cookbook. Even in the above recipe, the small amount of raisins should cause your dog no harm. If you are concerned, however, please omit.

Your dog will happily share your Thanksgiving dinner with you, but why not make him his own?

Roast Cornish Game Hen with Apple Sausage Stuffing and Gravy

INGREDIENTS

1 teaspoon vegetable oil

1 ounce (28 g) mild sausage, cut into small pieces

1 tablespoon diced celery

1 tablespoon diced apple

1 cup (50 g) bread cubes

¼ teaspoon poultry seasoning or ground sage

1 Cornish game hen, preferably fresh (about 1¼ pounds [565 g])

1 tablespoon all-purpose flour

¼ cup (55 ml) chicken broth

DIRECTIONS

1 Heat oil in small skillet over medium heat. Add sausage and cook, stirring frequently, until meat is brown, about 1 minute.

2 Add celery and apple and cook, stirring frequently, for another minute.

3 Place sausage mixture, bread cubes, and seasoning in a small bowl. Mix thoroughly to combine. Set aside.

4 Remove giblets* from bird's cavity. Rinse bird inside and out and pat dry with paper towels.

5 Fill bird's cavity loosely with stuffing.

6 Place stuffed bird on rack in small roasting pan. Roast in a preheated 450°F (230°C) oven for 15 minutes. Reduce oven temperature to 375°F (190°C) and roast another 45 minutes until juices run clear and internal temperature of the bird registers 180°F (85°C). (Cover bird with aluminum foil in last 15 to 20 minutes of cooking if breast is becoming too dark.)

7 Remove bird from rack and place on cutting board or platter to rest. Cover with foil.

8 Add flour to pan drippings; stir to incorporate flour and scrape up all the brown bits. Add chicken broth and cook and stir over medium heat until sauce comes to a boil and is smooth and thick, about 2 to 3 minutes. Makes 1 hen with stuffing.

9 To serve, cut meat from roasted game hen and place over dry dog food in dog bowl. Add stuffing and gravy. Serve with mashed potatoes and baked yams, if desired.

*Save giblets to make Giblet Gravy (page 53)

A DOG'S THANKSGIVING POEM

T is for Turkey, I want several slices.

H is for Ham, which you cut into dices.

A is for A Generous Scoop of mashed potatoes, and sweet potatoes, too.

N is for the NFL and the games that I'll view.

K is for Kibble, mix some with my dinner.

S is for Stuffing, with sausage—a winner.

G is for Gravy, please pour it on thick.

I is for Inhale, 'cause I lick it up quick.

V is for Very Full, the condition I'm in.

I is for my Interest in eating again.

N is for Nap, which I now need.

G is for Grateful that you are my person, which I am, indeed.

Sharing Thanksgiving Dinner with Your Dog

If preparing a special Thanksgiving entrée just for your dog is not your thing, that's okay. Just share some of yours, mixing with dry dog food as always and giving a total portion no bigger than usual. Here is a list of the types of foods you can include:

MEATS	VEGETABLES	STARCHES	SAUCES	DESSERTS (just a spoonful)
Turkey	Carrots	Potatoes	Gravy	Pumpkin pie
Ham	Squash	Rice	Cheese sauce	Apple pie
	Sweet potatoes	Stuffing		Pecan pie
	Green beans			Vanilla ice cream
	Peas			

Just a sliver, please, of this deliciously rich Christmas pie for your dog. And don't forget to leave some out for Santa Paws.

INGREDIENTS

1 teaspoon vegetable oil

¼ pound (115 g) ground pork or beef

1½ cups (340 g) prepared mincemeat

One 15-ounce (425 g) package ready-to-bake pie crusts

NOTE: Mincemeat contains a small amount of raisins. If you are concerned about your dog eating raisins (see "A Word about Raisins," p. 101), please do not make this dish for your dog.

MINCEMEAT PIES

DIRECTIONS

1 Heat oil in small skillet over medium-high heat. Add ground meat and cook, stirring frequently, until meat is brown, about 3 to 4 minutes. Drain meat on paper towel and cover with paper towel.

2 Divide each pie crust into 4 pieces, for a total of 8 pieces. On a floured surface, roll out each piece until it is big enough to cut out a 7-inch (17.5 cm) round.* Place a dough round into the bottoms of four 4-inch (10 cm) tart pans. Reserve remaining 4 rounds for pastry tops.

3 Meanwhile, place cooked meat and mincemeat in a small bowl. Mix thoroughly to combine. Spoon about ½ cup (115 g) mincemeat mixture into each pastry-lined tart pan.

4 For pastry tops, place pastry round on top of mincemeat-filled tart. Position small dog-shaped or bone-shaped cookie cutter in center of top pastry round. Lift up top pastry round and return to floured surface and cut out shape. Return top pastry to mincemeat-filled tart. Press together edges, fold under, and crimp.

5 Place filled tart pans on foil-lined baking sheet. Bake in a preheated 425°F (220°C) oven for 15 minutes until crust is golden brown. Cool on rack. Makes 4 tarts.

*The pastry rounds should be about 1 inch (2.5 cm) bigger than the tart shells you are using.

TIP

To make pastry doggies, use a dog-shaped cookie cutter to cut pastry scraps. Place on foil-lined baking sheet and bake at 425°F (220°C) for 5 to 8 minutes until golden brown. Cut out a sliver of red pepper to create a "winter scarf."

Neighbor Suzi makes handcrafted dog–treat wreaths for all the dogs, large and small, on her Christmas list. She shares the directions here.

DOG-TREAT WREATH

MATERIALS

Styrofoam craft wreath, 4 to 12 inches (10 to 30.5 cm)

Cardboard for larger wreaths

1-inch (2.5 cm) nonwired craft ribbon, 2 to 6 yards (1.8 to 5.5 m)

1-inch (2.5 cm) T-pins or short straight pins

Dog bone–shaped treats, such as Peanut Butter Bones (page 80) or GingerBones (page 81)

Silk greenery, flowers, and bows for decoration

Glue gun

DIRECTIONS

1 If using a 9-inch (22.5 cm) or larger Styrofoam wreath, place wreath on cardboard and trace around inner and outer edges, then cut out cardboard shape and glue cardboard onto back of Styrofoam. Allow to dry. (This will give the wreath greater strength.)

2 Cut a length of ribbon approximately 9 feet (2.7 m) for a 6-inch (15 cm) wreath and about 11 feet (3.4 m) for a 9-inch (22.5 cm) wreath.

3 Starting with the Styrofoam side of the wreath facing you, pin one end of the ribbon to the narrow edge (top) of the Styrofoam with long part of the ribbon away from you. Pull long end through center of wreath and wrap again over top and through center. (It is easier to handle the long end if you roll it up from the far end and pass the roll through each wrap.)

4 If making the wreath for a small dog, place a small bone on the front of the wreath at about the third wrap, half on the ribbon, and wrap over the right end of the bone, leaving the bone sticking out. Wrap over lower part of bone to secure it. Continue to wrap and place bones evenly around the wreath. Make sure you overlap the ribbon edges enough to cover the Styrofoam. Place the last bone even with the first one, leaving a space for the bow.

5 If making the wreath for a large dog, wrap wreath completely with ribbon. Attach a large dog bone with decorative ribbon at the end and proceed with directions.

6 When you have covered the entire wreath, turn wreath over and secure end of ribbon with a pin. Cut excess ribbon to about 1 inch (2.5 cm), turn the edge under, and glue it down. You can also secure it with a T-pin, making sure the pin is buried in the Styrofoam.

7 Attach silk leaves or greens with glue at the top front of the wreath and add a pretty bow. Make a wire loop on the back of the wreath to use as a hanger.

*Everyone knows that the wiry, energetic
Jack Russell terrier can jump sky high.
The JRT and others will hop to the dinner bowl
for this canine version of Hoppin' John,
a traditional dish served at Karamu, a feast
held during the African American observance
of Kwanzaa.*

HOPPIN' JACK RUSSELL

INGREDIENTS

5 cups (1.2 L) water, divided

½ cup (100 g) dried black-eyed peas

½ cup (100 g) uncooked white rice

1 teaspoon vegetable oil

¼ pound (115 g) kielbasa, cut into bite-sized pieces

½ cup (60 g) diced celery

DIRECTIONS

1 Bring 2 cups (450 ml) water to boil over high heat in a 2-quart (1.9 L) saucepan. Add black-eyed peas and boil for 2 minutes. Remove from heat and let sit, covered, for 1 hour.

2 Drain soaking water from peas. Add 2 cups (450 ml) fresh water to peas in pan and bring to boil over high heat. Reduce heat and let simmer, 15 to 20 minutes, until peas are tender. Drain and mash slightly.

3 Meanwhile, in another medium saucepan, bring 1 cup water to boil. Add rice, cover, reduce heat to medium-low, and cook for 15 to 20 minutes until all water is absorbed. Set aside.

4 Heat oil in a small skillet over medium heat. Add kielbasa and celery and cook, stirring frequently, until kielbasa is cooked, about 5 minutes. Combine kielbasa mixture with black-eyed peas. Makes about 1 quart (0.95 L). Serve with rice over dry dog food.

CHAPTER 7

ETHNIC SPECIALTIES

Whether dogs are proud of their own ethnic heritage or embrace that of their human family, they enjoy ethnic food just like everyone else. From English to Asian, Italian, and Jewish, popular dog breeds across the country share their favorite recipes.

From Akitas to Shih Tzus,
dogs of Asian heritage
will want to chow-chow down
on this tasty stir-fry.

BEEF AND BEAN STIR-FRY

INGREDIENTS

1 tablespoon vegetable oil

¼ pound (115 g) flank steak, cut into thin strips

1 cup (100 g) cut green beans

¼ cup (30 g) diced red pepper

½ cup (115 ml) beef broth

1 tablespoon hoisin sauce

½ teaspoon ground ginger

DIRECTIONS

1 Heat oil in small skillet over medium-high heat. Add steak strips and cook, stirring frequently, until meat is brown, about 1 to 2 minutes.

2 Add beans and pepper and cook, stirring frequently, another 1 to 2 minutes.

3 Combine broth, hoisin sauce, and ginger in a measuring cup and add to pan. Cook an additional 1 to 2 minutes. Makes about 2 cups. Serve with rice over dry dog food. Garnish with peanuts, if desired.

Latkes are potato pancakes traditionally served at Hanukkah. Spin a dreidel and share some with your dog.

LATKES WITH YOGURT AND HAROSET

INGREDIENTS

2 large potatoes, peeled, cooked, and grated

1 egg, slightly beaten

1 tablespoon all-purpose flour

½ teaspoon baking powder

1 tablespoon vegetable oil

DIRECTIONS

1   Place grated potatoes in a strainer over a bowl to drain off liquid (can be done early in day or night before).

2   Place potatoes, egg, flour, and baking powder in a large bowl. Mix thoroughly to combine. Form into small pancakes.

3   Meanwhile, heat oil on griddle or small skillet over medium-high heat. Add pancakes and cook until golden brown on both sides, about 1 to 2 minutes per side. Makes 8 to 12 pancakes. Serve over dry dog food with a dollop of plain yogurt and a spoonful of Haroset (recipe follows).

HAROSET

INGREDIENTS

1 apple, diced

½ cup (60 g) chopped walnuts

2 tablespoons honey

DIRECTIONS

Place all ingredients in a small bowl and mix to combine.

Many dog breeds originated in the British Isles. This is a dogified version of an English specialty.

DOGGIE-BY-THE-SEA FISH PIE

DIRECTIONS

1 Bring milk just to the boiling point in a small skillet. Add fish fillets, reduce heat to medium-low, and allow to simmer until fish is cooked, about 8 to 10 minutes. Remove fish from pan and reserve liquid in skillet.

2 Flake fish with fork and place in bottom of greased 8-inch (20 cm) baking dish.

3 Top with egg slices and parsley.

4 Meanwhile, melt butter in 1-quart (0.95 L) saucepan over medium heat. Stir in flour to make a paste. Slowly add the cooking liquid, stirring to incorporate flour. Cook, stirring constantly, until sauce thickens, about 2 to 3 minutes.

5 Pour milk sauce over fish and eggs in baking dish. Top with mashed potatoes, covering entire dish.

6 Place baking dish in a preheated 375°F (190°C) oven and bake for 30 minutes. Makes about 1 quart (0.95 L). Serve over dry dog food with cooked spinach and carrots, if desired.

INGREDIENTS

½ cup (115 ml) milk

½ pound (225 g) cod fillets

2 hard-cooked eggs, sliced

2 teaspoons chopped parsley

2 teaspoons butter

2 teaspoons all-purpose flour

2 cups (420 g) mashed potatoes

Mangia, mangia.

This traditional Italian soup is full of good ingredients for dogs.

MUTT'S MINESTRONE

DIRECTIONS

1. Heat oil in an 8-quart (7.6 L) stockpot over medium-high heat. Add beef and cook, stirring frequently, until meat is brown, about 8 minutes. Stir in oregano and basil.

2. Add water, beef broth, tomatoes with juice, and cannellini beans. Bring to boil over high heat.

3. Add potatoes, carrots, and celery. Reduce heat to medium and cook, stirring occasionally, for 10 minutes.

4. Add ditalini and zucchini and cook, stirring frequently, for an additional 10 minutes.

5. Remove from heat and stir in cabbage. Makes about 8 quarts (7.6 L). (Recipe may be doubled.) Serve over dry dog food.

INGREDIENTS

2 tablespoons vegetable oil

1 pound (450 g) ground beef

1 teaspoon dried oregano

1 teaspoon dried basil

1 quart (0.95 L) water

2 cups (450 ml) beef broth

One 28-ounce (828 ml) can diced tomatoes in juice

One 19-ounce (540 g) can cannellini beans, drained, rinsed, and slightly mashed

2 potatoes, peeled and chopped

2 carrots, peeled and sliced

2 celery stalks, chopped

1 cup (150 g) ditalini

2 zucchini, chopped

½ head cabbage, shredded

Ay, Chihuahua.
Any hot-blooded **perro**
is going to love this one.

CHILI BEEF 'N' BEANS

INGREDIENTS

1 tablespoon vegetable oil

½ pound (225 g) ground beef

1 teaspoon chili powder

One 14½-ounce (429 ml) can diced tomatoes in juice

One 14½-ounce (411 g) can kidney beans, drained, rinsed, and slightly mashed

1 small zucchini, chopped

½ cup (75 g) frozen corn

DIRECTIONS

1 Heat oil in large skillet over medium heat. Add ground beef and cook, stirring frequently until meat is brown, about 2 to 3 minutes.

2 Add chili powder and cook, stirring, for 30 seconds.

3 Add tomatoes with juice and beans. Cook, stirring occasionally, for 5 minutes.

4 Add zucchini and cook, stirring occasionally, for an additional 5 minutes.

5 Remove from heat. Stir in corn. Makes about 1 quart (0.95 L). Serve over dry dog food with rice, shredded cheese, and baked tortilla strips, if desired.

*You don't have to be a Weimaraner
or a wiener dog to enjoy a good schnitzel.*

WIENERSCHNITZEL

DIRECTIONS

1 With bread crumbs in a plate or shallow dish, coat veal slices on both sides.

2 Heat oil in a small nonstick skillet over medium heat. Add veal slices and cook until cooked through and golden brown on both sides, about 2 minutes per side. Cut into bite-sized pieces and serve over dry dog food with cooked carrots and mashed potatoes, if desired. Makes about ½ cup (150 g).

INGREDIENTS

¼ cup (30 g) plain bread crumbs

¼ pound (115 g) sliced veal, pounded thin

2 tablespoons vegetable oil

CHAPTER 8

SPECIAL DIETS FOR SPECIAL NEEDS

Sometimes disease or some other condition may demand that you provide your fur-friend with a special diet. Of course, your vet is the one to diagnose your dog's problem, and in most cases, the special diet will be accompanied by medical treatment. When your dog is on a special diet, it is especially important to give him a vitamin and mineral supplement. This chapter focuses on several common ailments afflicting dogs and the home-cooked diets that can help manage these diseases or disorders.

You can still make a tasty meal for your big-hearted creature when he has heart problems.

HEART-SMART DIET

DIRECTIONS

1 Bring water to boil over high heat in a 3-quart (2.8 L) saucepan. Add rice, reduce heat to medium-low, cover, and cook for 15 to 20 minutes until all water has been absorbed. Set aside.

2 Meanwhile, heat oil in small skillet over medium heat. Add ground beef and cook, stirring frequently, until meat is brown and cooked through, about 4 to 5 minutes.

3 Stir meat into rice. Makes about 1 quart (0.95 L). Serve with h/d (heart diet) dry dog food.

INGREDIENTS

2½ cups (565 ml) water

1¼ cups (250 g) uncooked white rice

2 tablespoons vegetable oil

½ pound (225 g) lean ground beef

Common Symptoms of Heart Disease in Dogs

- Shortness of breath
- Lethargy or sluggishness

See a vet immediately if dog has labored breathing or frequent coughing, or if it collapses.

Kidney disease in dogs can usually be managed with a combination of medicine and diet.

INGREDIENTS

1 pound (450 g) salmon*

1½ quarts (1.4 L) water

4 potatoes, peeled and cubed

4 carrots, peeled and cubed

*Or, use 1 pound cooked chicken breasts or a combination of cooked chicken and eggs, depending on the type of kidney disease your dog has. Your vet will let you know whether a fish diet or a chicken diet is appropriate.

Common Symptoms of Kidney Disease in Dogs

◄ Drinking lots of water

▬ Frequent urination

▬ Urine that is pale yellow to colorless

See a vet immediately if dog vomits or excretes undigested food.

KIDNEY-CARE DIET

DIRECTIONS

1 Place salmon on foil-lined baking sheet, and place in a preheated 400°F (200°C) oven. Bake until fish is cooked through and flakes easily, about 20 minutes. Let fish cool slightly, then flake, picking through fish carefully to remove all bones.

2 Meanwhile, bring water to a boil in a large saucepan. Add potatoes and carrots and cook until vegetables are tender, about 15 to 20 minutes. Drain and mash.

3 In a large bowl, combine vegetables and flaked fish. Makes about 1½ quarts (1.4 L). Serve with k/d (kidney diet) dry dog food.

DOGGEREL

My own Gwennie was diagnosed with kidney failure about six months before she succumbed to the disease. At the time, kidney disease could be diagnosed only through blood analysis, and the diagnosis could be made definitively only when kidneys were at least 75 percent or more compromised. The diagnosis is made even more difficult because the common symptoms mimic those of other diseases, notably diabetes and Cushing's disease.

Now, fortunately, kidney disease can be diagnosed much earlier through a simple urine test. Dogs can be put on a combination of medicine and diet that can, it is hoped, help prolong their lives.

When Gwennie was diagnosed, I purchased both the k/d dry dog food and canned food (typically a fish-potato diet) at my vet's office. Gwennie—always an eager eater—smelled something fishy and would have none of it, even if I hand-fed her. So, with the help of my vet, I devised my own fish-potato stew, to which I added carrots for greater appetite appeal, and mixed it with the k/d dry dog food. Gwennie then thought she was getting something special, which she was not about to share with her brother Humphrey.

On this diet, Gwennie's condition stabilized for several months. She was able to live comfortably and happily (well, she was always happy) with the disease another six months until, the disease too far advanced for even medicine and diet, she went into acute kidney failure and died in my arms.

Many dogs exhibit allergy symptoms, and some breeds are more susceptible than others. Some dogs, like people, are plagued only mildly and seasonally with allergies, whereas others are tormented year-round. This diet will help you determine which foods your dog may be allergic to.

ALLERGY DIET

DIRECTIONS

Heat oil in a skillet over medium heat. Add duck or venison and cook, stirring frequently, until meat is brown and cooked through, about 4 to 5 minutes. Makes about 1 quart (0.95 L). Serve with a dry dog food formulated for dogs with allergy problems.

INGREDIENTS

2 tablespoons vegetable oil

1 pound (450 g) duck or venison, cut into bite-sized pieces

Common Symptoms
of Allergies in Dogs

→ Frequent to incessant scratching
or rubbing

→ Redness or welts on the skin

→ Discoloration of fur, especially
around the ears, eyes, mouth,
and/or paws

See a vet immediately if dog
begins to lose hair or welts
become inflamed or infected.

Ascertaining What
Your Dog Is Allergic To

The point of the Allergy Diet is to determine what food or foods
your dog may be allergic to.

→ Start with a blank slate—a food he has never eaten before, such as
duck or venison. (It used to be that lamb was the protein of choice
in an allergy diet, but lamb-and-rice dog food is now quite common.
So start with duck or venison, either one of which your dog will, no
doubt, be delighted to find on his menu.)

→ Serve the duck or venison with a dry dog food formulated for
allergy-prone dogs (check with your vet) for two months to make
sure your dog is symptom-free.

→ Then add one ingredient, such as plain cooked rice or cooked
carrots, and serve that combination for two weeks. (This diet
requires patience.)

→ Continue adding ingredients every two weeks until you see the
allergic symptoms return. Then you have identified the offending
food or foods.

→ Eliminate the problem foods altogether from your dog's diet, and
make appropriate substitutions.

Foods Dogs Are Frequently
Allergic To

IF YOUR DOG SEEMS ALLERGIC TO	THEN
Wheat flour or products	Substitute rice flour or nonwheat products
Dairy products	Eliminate, or substitute soy-based products

Other Foods to Watch Out For

Some foods can be out-and-out lethal to dogs.
Others can be dangerous, though usually only
when ingested in large quantities. The ASPCA's
Animal Poison Control Center provides this short
but important list:

NEVER
Chocolate
Macadamia nuts

RESTRICT (and monitor for any problems)
Onions and related family members (e.g.,
scallions or green onions, shallots, garlic)
Raisins and green grapes
(see "A Word about Raisins," page 101)

Sometimes your dog has an upset stomach and the result is—well, you know—vomiting and diarrhea. Put him on a bland diet for a day or two and he should be good as new.

TUMMY-UPSET DIET

INGREDIENTS

1 quart (0.95 L) water, divided

1 cup (200 g) uncooked white rice

1 pound (450 g) skinless, boneless chicken breasts*

*Or, use 1 pound ground beef, cooked.

DIRECTIONS

1 Bring 2 cups (450 ml) water to boil over high heat in a 3-quart (2.8 L) saucepan. Add rice, reduce heat to medium-low, cover, and cook for 15 to 20 minutes until all water has been absorbed. Set aside.

2 Meanwhile, bring remaining 2 cups (450 ml) water to boil over high heat in a shallow saucepan. Add chicken breasts, reduce heat to medium, and cook for 15 to 20 minutes until chicken is cooked through. Remove chicken from water. Let cool slightly, and cut into bite-sized pieces.

3 Stir chicken into rice. Makes about 1 quart (0.95 L).

Tips for Tending to an Upset Tummy

➤ Serve the above mixture in small amounts four to six times during the day. As the dog is able to keep the food down and digest it normally, add a little dry dog food.

➤ Keep the dog on this bland diet for twenty-four to forty-eight hours, until normal digestion returns; then gradually resume feeding him his regular food at his usual feeding times.

➤ Other bland foods to consider include Cream of Wheat cereal, cottage cheese, and hard-cooked eggs.

Common Symptoms of Stomach Upset in Dogs

➤ Vomiting

➤ Diarrhea

See a vet immediately if dog has violent vomiting and/or diarrhea, especially if the vomit or excrement includes undigested food and/or blood, or if the dog is lethargic.

CONFESSIONS OF A COUCH POOCH-TATO

I confess, there are two things I love: Eating and napping, preferably on a comfy couch where I can snore as loud as I want and at the same time keep one watchful eye on my people and one ear cocked for someone to open the refrigerator door.

Since my mom got this cookbook, I've been livin' large. And gettin' larger. Uh-oh. I love my mom's cooking, but she's been feeding me too much. But I always lick my bowl clean just to show her how much I appreciate everything she does for me.

Then one day she told me I was looking pretty chunky. Who? *Moi?* What makes her think I'm overweight? She says it's because she can't feel my ribs. "Ok, Buster," she says, "we're putting you on a diet and we're getting your tail in gear." What's this? Diet? Exercise? Yep. Next thing I know she's measuring my food to make sure she doesn't overfeed me (doggone it!). And every day we go for a walk. At first we just started out by strolling around the block. Now we walk three miles every day. And on Sundays, we go to the park and I get to romp and play with my friends.

I am slimmer and trimmer now, and my mom is happy because she says I will live a long and healthy life. That's good. That gives me a lot more time to take naps on the couch.

FOR ADDITIONAL NUTRITION AND VETERINARY INFORMATION:

www.allaboutpets.org.uk

www.animalhealthcare.ca

www.aspca.org

www.canismajor.com

www.dog.com

www.dogsincanada.com

www.ivis.org

www.petdiets.com

www.pethealthcare.co.uk

www.petplanet.co.uk

www.thedogscene.co.uk

www.veterinarypartner.com

www.vetinfo.com

www.vin.com

FOR PUBLICATIONS:

Canine Nutrition: What Every Owner, Breeder, and Trainer Should Know by Lowell Ackerman, DVM. Published by Alpine Publications, 1999.

Dog Health & Nutrition for Dummies by M. Christine Zink, DVM. Published by For Dummies, June 1, 2001.

Feeding Your Dog for Life: The Real Facts about Proper Nutrition by Diane Morgan. Published by Doral Publishing, April 2002.

Your Dog – A Newsletter for Dog Owners. Published by Tufts Media. For subscription information, call (800) 829-5116.

FOR PREMIUM-QUALITY DRY DOG FOOD:

Visit a fine pet supply store

Check online by searching "dog food."

FOR DOG RESCUE ORGANIZATIONS:

www.akc.org

www.animalrescuers.co.uk

www.doggiedirectory.com

www.dogpages.org.uk

www.i-love-dogs.com/search/directory/Dog
    Rescue/Rescue in Canada

www.petfinders.org

www.rescuers.com

Check your local animal shelter

FOR COOKING INGREDIENTS AND SUPPLIES:

www.bakerscatalogue.com
rice flour and other specialty flours. Or check your local health food store or call (800) 827-6836.

www.cookiecutter.com
cookie cutters in a various shapes and sizes.

www.penzeys.com
high-quality dry herbs and spices at reasonable prices. Or call (800) 741-7787.

Smiling Dog
Mutt Muffin Molds (large cat, bone, and fire hydrant shapes) are available at fine pet supply stores. Or visit www.smilingdog.net or call (800) 816-PETS.

ABOUT THE AUTHOR

Donna Twichell Roberts is a food writer and public relations consultant. After having real jobs for twenty years at a Fortune 50 food company and an advertising and public relations agency, Donna started her own business, Advantage Communications, from her home. In this relatively stress-free environment, she happily represents a number of wonderful clients. Her only coworkers have been dogs, who, frankly, do not provide much assistance but keep their mouths shut unless, of course, the UPS driver rings the doorbell. Donna lives in Brookfield, Connecticut, and is owned by Katie, a West Highland White Terrier.

Katie G. McGee is a shy little lady of a certain age. She was born an unknown number of years ago in a puppy mill and spent most of her life as a puppy-mill mama. Then this scared little dog with no name, only an ear tattoo, was saved by Westie Rescue of Missouri. Three years ago, Katie entered Donna's house and heart and has been loved and cared for ever since. Her only job is to nap on the dog bed next to her mom's computer.

Blake Swihart provided his food styling expertise to this book. An executive chef, Blake graduated from the Culinary Institute of America. He manages his own company, FoodService Solutions, which provides full-service marketing support to many organizations and companies. On the board of directors of the International Association of Culinary Professionals, Blake lives in Chester Springs, Pennsylvania, and is owned by Izzy the Airedale.

Acknowledgments

Thank you to Leslie Medina Scocca, who got me started on cooking for my dogs, and Barbara Albright, who recommended me to the publishers for the project.

To John Eddy, thank you for your understanding, enthusiastic support, and so much more.

To sisters Bonnie Inscho and Becky Twichell and to friends Donna Carlton, Lisa Jones, Dee Klarich, Carol Lally, David Magill, Marion O'Connor, Courtney Romano, and Kathy Scherb: Thank you for so many years of love, laughs, support, and encouragement. A particular thanks goes to Blake Swihart for his enduring friendship and food styling expertise, without which this book would not be so beautiful. And to friend Chris Clark for her recipe testing and kitchen assistance.

Of course, this cookbook would not be possible without scores of eager dogs who, over the years, have woofed down stews and begged, sat up, offered paw, and rolled over for cookies. For this project, I owe a special thanks to Golden, a blond cocker, and his mom, Mary Linardo; Gabriella and Buddy, both black labs, and their mom, Suzanne Nassar. And to neighbor Suzi Diehl, who delivered recipe samples to Gabriella and Buddy, who designed the dog bone holiday wreaths, and who is fun to visit because she almost always has a kitchenful of puppies she is fostering for Guiding Eyes for the Blind.

And, of course, to my own Katie, who sometimes taste-tested a different recipe every night. I am happy to report that she never had any tummy upsets or intestinal trouble from such a varied diet. In fact, every night she would run out to the kitchen at suppertime and sit up on her hind end as if to say, "What's for dinner tonight, Mom?" She refuses to name a favorite.

And to all my online friends at The Westie Connection, Westie Express, the remarkable people at Westie Rescue of Missouri, and to dog lovers everywhere who rescue, transport, foster, and adopt dogs who need good homes.

To my own vet, Dr. Michael Dattner, for his guidance on certain sections in this book, along with Dr. Silke Bogart and the staff at Brookfield Animal Hospital for their expert and sensitive care of my dogs over the years.

To the folks at Tail Waggers in Bethel, Connecticut, for the loan of dog bowls and cookie jars, and the friends at Brookfield Craft Center in Brookfield, Connecticut, for the loan of handcrafted dog-breed bowls.

And finally, to Mary Ann Hall and Regina Grenier and others at Rockport Publishers for making this such an enjoyable experience.